Color Me Productive

Intuitive Publishing
209 S. Shady Shores
Ste 300-155
Lake Dallas, TX 75065

ISBN: 978-0692549568

Color Me Productive

Playful Distractions to Inspire Your Workday

Illustrated by Audrey Christie McLaughlin

Intuitive Publishing

Introduction

Why an adult coloring book?

Did you love coloring as a child? Coloring is an activity we typically associate with children. Studies show that the practice of coloring for adults generates wellness and quiets the mind, while stimulating brain areas related to motor skills, the senses and creativity. When you are relaxed and more creative you give your productivity the ability to soar!

How does this make me more productive + creative?

There are many studies that indicate that coloring can reduce stress, improve creativity and lead to better production at work. Psychologists say that when coloring, we activate both logic and creativity, using both cerebral hemispheres while coloring our masterpieces.

Tips + Tricks

Don't overthink coloring! Just grab your coloring utensil of choice and get going! Using crayons may be difficult due to the portable size of this coloring book. Colored pencils or fine tipped markers will be optimal for this book. Try taking 10-15 minute coloring breaks every 90 minutes during your work day. Don't worry if you aren't able to complete an image the beauty is you can work on a single image for a period of time or choose a simpler image and work until completion.

What are mandalas?

Mandala is a Sanskrit word for circle. Historically, mandalas are a common tool used in meditation aids and for many other uses as well. They are often geometric and symmetrical, and vary in complexity.

In some religions, the mandala is a sacred symbol used for healing and for reflection of the outside world.

The coloring diagrams in this book are all illustrated mandalas, each created with specific intentions. Once you begin to color the mandala becomes your very own container for anything you need it to be in the moment.

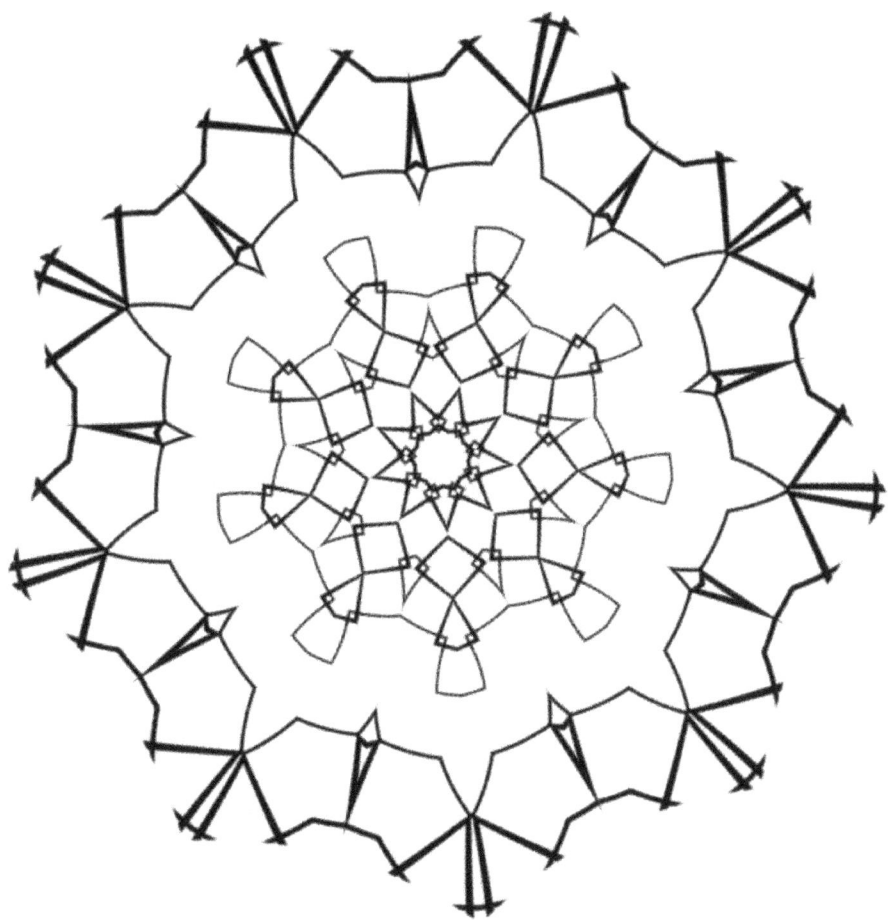

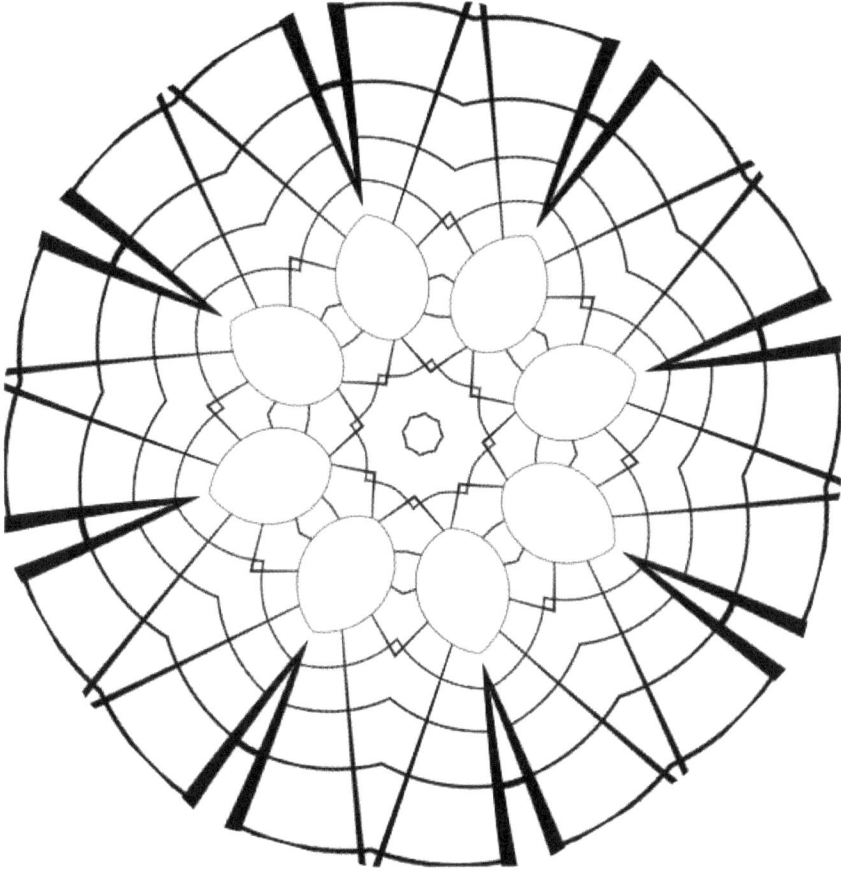

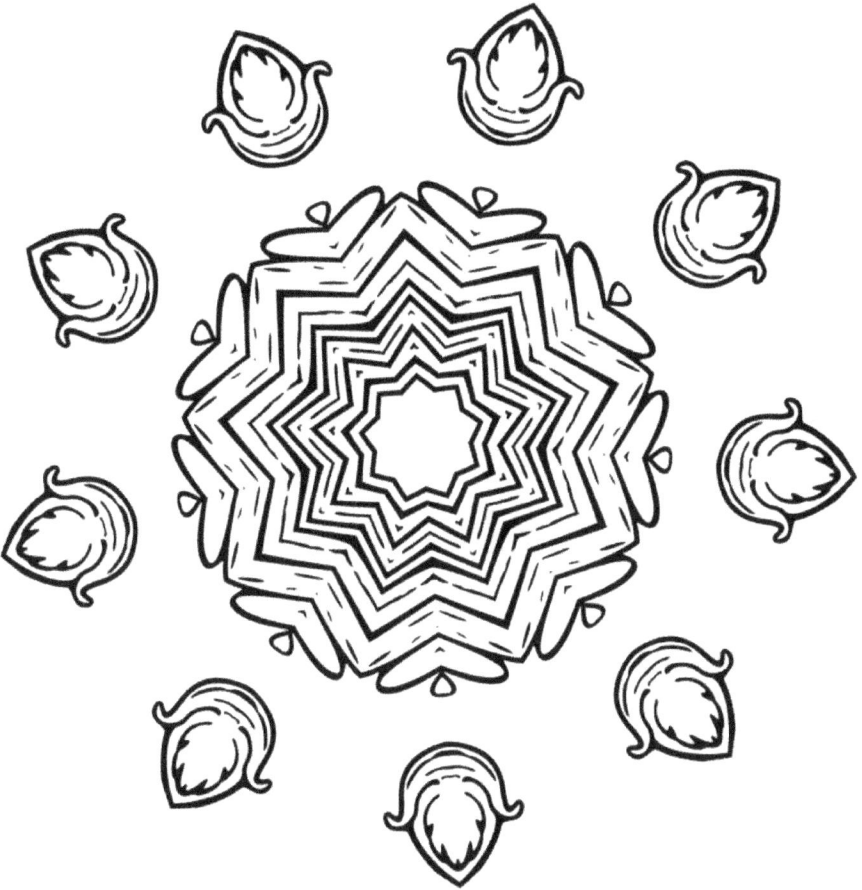

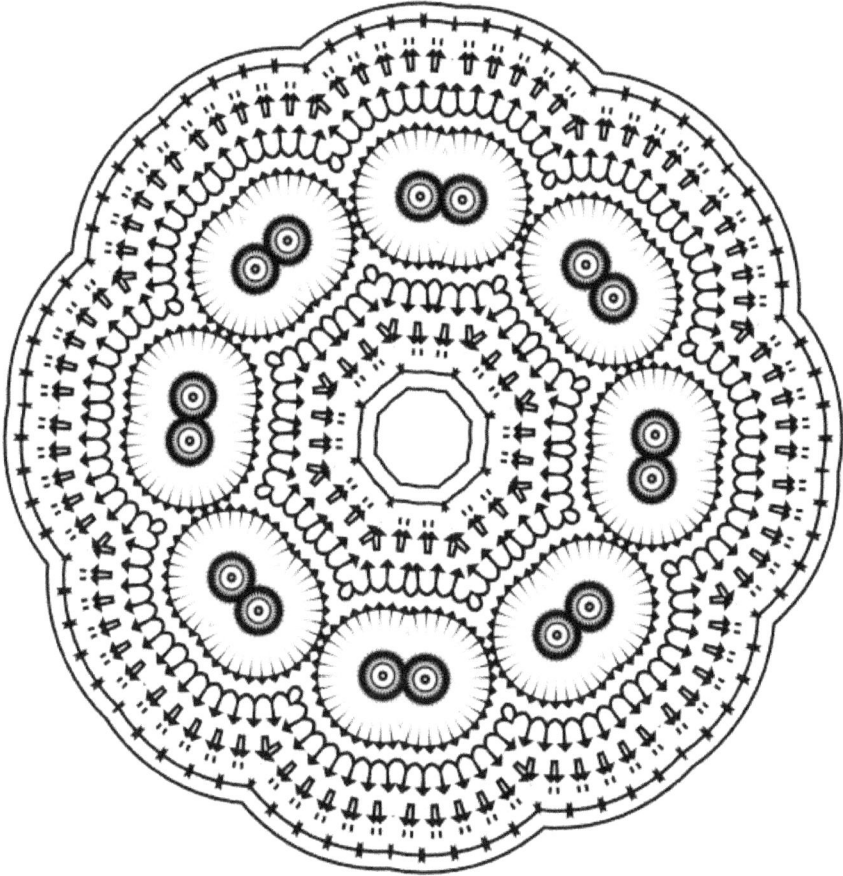

About Audrey Christie McLaughlin

Audrey Christie McLaughlin is a wife, mama, yogi, and fan of football, art and general positivity.

Professionally, Audrey is a social media marketer and business growth strategist. She helps her clients grow local and online businesses and bring in more customers, clients and patients.

Audrey uses art and coloring in her own business to encourage creativity and foster productivity for herself and her team.

You can find out more about Audrey and Intuitive Marketing Genius at www.IntuitiveMarketingGenius.com or reach out to her directly at Audrey@IntuitiveMarketingGenius.com.

www.ingramcontent.com/pod-product-compliance
Lightning Source LLC
Chambersburg PA
CBHW060638210326
41520CB00010B/1647